INDIGENOUS BIOGRAPHIES

# Maria Tallchief

## Prima Ballerina

FOCUS READERS® BEACON

by Katrina M. Phillips

www.focusreaders.com



Focus Readers is distributed by North Star Editions:
sales@northstareditions.com | 888-417-0195

Produced for Focus Readers by Red Line Editorial.

Photographs ©: AP Images, cover, 1, 13, 16, 22; New York Public Library, 4, 6, 29; Shutterstock Images, 8; Evening Standard/Hulton Archive/Getty Images, 11; University of Tulsa Archive, 15; Bettmann/Getty Images, 19; Baron/Hulton Archive/Getty Images, 21; Jack Mitchell/Archive Photos/Getty Images, 25; Stacia Timonere/Hulton Archive/Getty Images, 26

**Library of Congress Cataloging-in-Publication Data**
Names: Phillips, Katrina M., author.
Title: Maria Tallchief: prima ballerina / by Katrina M. Phillips.
Description: Mendota Heights, MN: Focus Readers, [2026]. | Series: Indigenous biographies | Includes bibliographical references and index. | Audience: Grades 2-3
Identifiers: LCCN 2024059753 (print) | LCCN 2024059754 (ebook) | ISBN 9798889985051 (hardcover) | ISBN 9798889986591 (paperback) | ISBN 9798889985686 (ebook pdf) | ISBN 9798889985372 (hosted ebook)
Subjects: LCSH: Tallchief, Maria--Juvenile literature. | Indian ballerinas--United States--Biography--Juvenile literature. | Osage Indians--United States--Biography--Juvenile literature. | LCGFT: Literature. | Biographies.
Classification: LCC GV1785.T32 P45 2026 (print) | LCC GV1785.T32 (ebook) | DDC 792.802/8092 [B]--dc23/eng/20250120
LC record available at https://lccn.loc.gov/2024059753
LC ebook record available at https://lccn.loc.gov/2024059754

Printed in the United States of America
Mankato, MN
012026

## About the Author

Dr. Katrina M. Phillips (Red Cliff Ojibwe) is a writer, researcher, and history professor. She's written several children's books about Native histories and cultures, including *Indigenous Peoples' Day* and *I Am on Indigenous Land*. She and her husband live in Minnesota with their two sons and their goofy dog.

# Table of Contents

# THE NUTCRACKER

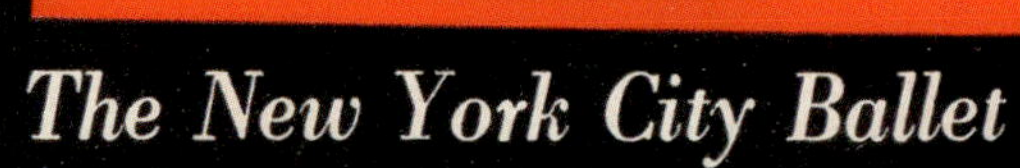

*The New York City Ballet*

CHAPTER 1

# Creating a Tradition

The New York City Ballet started **performing** a new work in 1954. It was called *The Nutcracker*. It was popular in Russia. But it had rarely appeared in America. George Balanchine wanted to change that.

**The New York City Ballet's 1954 version of *The Nutcracker* was made for American audiences.**

**Maria Tallchief poses as the Sugar Plum Fairy in *The Nutcracker* in 1954.**

He was a famous **choreographer**. Balanchine made a new *Nutcracker*.

The Sugar Plum Fairy is an important part of *The Nutcracker*. Balanchine needed a strong dancer. He needed a dancer he could trust.

So, he chose Maria Tallchief to be the Sugar Plum Fairy.

Tallchief was an Osage dancer. She was the first American **prima ballerina**. Her dancing in *The Nutcracker* amazed audiences. One writer said it was like magic. Tallchief helped *The Nutcracker* become a US holiday **tradition**.

## Did You Know?

Maria Tallchief was the first **Indigenous** prima ballerina.

TALL CHIEF
WHY
KILLERS FLOWER MOON
EXHIBIT HERE

CHAPTER 2

# Becoming Maria Tallchief

Elizabeth Marie Tall Chief was born on January 24, 1925. She grew up in Fairfax, Oklahoma, on the Osage **reservation**. Her family called her Betty Marie. Her sister, Marjorie, was born a year later.

**Elizabeth Marie Tall Chief's father owned the movie theater in Fairfax, Oklahoma.**

Their father, Alexander, was Osage. Their mother, Ruth, was Scots-Irish.

Betty Marie had her first dance lesson at three years old. Marjorie started lessons a year later. Ruth wanted her daughters to be famous dancers. But she didn't believe they could be famous in Oklahoma. In 1933, Ruth moved the family to Los Angeles, California.

In Los Angeles, Ruth tried to find the best teachers for her daughters. The sisters were 11 and 12 years

**Marjorie (left) and Betty Marie remained close their whole lives.**

old when they started studying with Bronislava Nijinska. She had been a famous ballerina. Betty Marie danced in Nijinska's *Chopin Concerto* when she was 15.

Betty Marie finished high school in 1942. But she continued dancing.

She joined a **company** called the Ballet Russe de Monte Carlo. She was only 17 years old.

At the time, the most famous ballet dancers came from Russia. Some people said Betty Marie should change her name. They thought she should become Maria

## Did You Know?

**Ballet was created in Italy in the 1400s. By the early 1900s, it was most popular in France and Russia.**

**Many of the best American ballet dancers joined the Ballet Russe.**

Tallchieva. This would make her sound more like a Russian ballerina. Betty Marie refused. She did not want to change her Osage last name. But she agreed to dance as Maria Tallchief.

TOPIC SPOTLIGHT

# The Five Moons

There were five Indigenous ballet dancers known as the "Five Moons." All five were from Oklahoma. All danced for the Ballet Russe. The most famous were Maria and Marjorie Tallchief.

Rosella Hightower was the oldest. She was Choctaw. Hightower later started her own dance school in France. Yvonne Chouteau was Shawnee and Cherokee. She joined the Ballet Russe at just 14 years old. Moscelyne Larkin was Shawnee-Peoria. She led a festival for the Five Moons in 1957. She held another in 1967. The Five Moons have been honored for helping make ballet popular in America.

**Moscelyne Larken (left), Marjorie Tallchief (back, center), Yvonne Chouteau (front, center), and Rosella Hightower dance together in 1957.**

YOU ARE WELCOME TO TAKE WITH
A PIECE OF THIS
CHRISTIAN SCIENCE

CHAPTER 3

# Bringing Ballet to America

Many choreographers worked with the Ballet Russe. George Balanchine came to the Ballet Russe in 1944. He began creating dances for the company.

**Maria Tallchief prepares to perform in a ballet in 1944.**

Tallchief danced in many of his works. Audiences loved them.

The Ballet Russe was successful. However, it was very European. Balanchine wanted to start an American ballet tradition. He helped create the Ballet Society in 1946. The company offered

## Did You Know?

**Ballet was not always popular in the United States. Tallchief and the Ballet Society helped change that.**

Ballet requires strength, timing, flexibility, and gracefulness.

**subscriptions** to its ballets. This meant more people could go to the ballet. Today, it is known as the New York City Ballet.

Tallchief and Balanchine fell in love as they worked together.

They got married in 1946. Together, they changed the world of ballet. Tallchief made history in 1947. She was the first American to dance with the Paris Opera Ballet.

In 1949, Balanchine created a major new ballet. The dance was based on Igor Stravinsky's *The Firebird*. Tallchief danced the role of the Firebird. This role became one of the hardest roles for a ballerina. The audience leapt to their feet when the ballet was over. Tallchief

**Tallchief performed some dance steps in *The Firebird* that had never been done before.**

later said it seemed like the theater had become a football stadium.

Newspapers loved Tallchief's performance, too. They said she was dazzling, brilliant, and superior. By 1953, she was the most famous ballet dancer in the world.

CHAPTER 4

# A Dancer's Legacy

Maria Tallchief may have been famous around the world. But she did not forget where she came from. In 1953, the Osage Nation in Oklahoma held a celebration for her. She received many gifts.

**Maria Tallchief wears a traditional Osage blanket at an Osage Nation celebration in 1954.**

She was also given the name *Wa.xthe.thomba*. It means "Woman of Two Worlds."

Tallchief remained at the New York City Ballet until 1958. She performed as its prima ballerina. Tallchief retired from ballet in 1966. She was 41 years old.

However, Tallchief did not leave the dance world. She moved to Chicago, Illinois. From 1973 to 1979, she directed the Chicago Lyric Opera Ballet. She and her

**Tallchief performed *The Firebird* into the 1960s.**

sister, Marjorie, created the Chicago City Ballet in 1981.

Maria Tallchief received several major awards during her lifetime.

Tallchief was involved with ballet for the rest of her life.

She was given a **Kennedy Center Honor** in 1996. Then in 1999, she received a National Medal of the Arts and Humanities. That is the highest award an artist can receive in the United States.

Maria Tallchief died in 2013. She was 88 years old. The little girl from Oklahoma had become a star. She had danced around the world. And she had helped bring ballet to America. Tallchief was still honored into the 2020s. The Osage Nation held Maria and Marjorie Tallchief Day on October 29, 2023.

## Did You Know?

**In 2023, Tallchief was featured on a US quarter.**

# Focus Questions

*Write your answers on a separate piece of paper.*

1. Write a letter to a friend about the Five Moons.
2. Would you change your name to fit in with a group? Why or why not?
3. Where did Maria Tallchief grow up?
   - A. Oklahoma
   - B. California
   - C. New York
4. Why might Maria Tallchief have been given the name *Wa.xthe.thomba*?
   - A. Tallchief stayed in her hometown when she became a star.
   - B. Tallchief was part of both the world of ballet and the world of Osage Nation.
   - C. Tallchief never fully succeeded in the world of ballet.

**5.** What does **superior** mean in this book?

*Newspapers loved Tallchief's performance, too. They said she was dazzling, brilliant, and **superior**.*

**A.** not well-known
**B.** very forgettable
**C.** one of the best

**6.** What does **celebration** mean in this book?

*In 1953, the Osage Nation in Oklahoma held a **celebration** for her. She received many gifts.*

**A.** an event people watch for fun
**B.** an event when someone's born
**C.** an event honoring someone

*Answer key on page 32.*

# Glossary

**choreographer**
A person who creates dance routines.

**company**
A group of professional dancers.

**Indigenous**
Native to a region, or belonging to ancestors who lived in a region before colonists arrived.

**Kennedy Center Honor**
An honor given to people in the performing arts. It often recognizes a lifetime of contributions to American culture.

**performing**
Putting on a play, concert, dance, or other kind of entertainment.

**prima ballerina**
The main female dancer in a ballet or ballet company.

**reservation**
Land set aside by the US government for a Native nation.

**subscriptions**
Payments that allow people to attend a certain number of shows.

**tradition**
A way of doing something that is passed down over many years.

# To Learn More

## BOOKS

Berrios, Frank. *The Story of Misty Copeland.* Callisto Publishing, 2021.

Day, Christine. *She Persisted: Maria Tallchief.* Philomel Books, 2021.

Meikle, Olivia, and Katie Nelson. *The Book of Sisters: Biographies of Incredible Siblings Through History.* St. Martin's Press, 2022.

## NOTE TO EDUCATORS

Visit **www.focusreaders.com** to find links and resources related to this title.

# Index



**Answer Key:** 1. Answers will vary; 2. Answers will vary; 3. A; 4. B; 5. C; 6. C